The Birds in My Life

By Supreme Master Ching Hai

Inspired by the Birds

Compiled by Supreme Master Ching Hai

Dedicated to All Earth's Co-inhabitants

With Love

4

FOR:
Prince Eleganto
Gentino
Amigo
Mimi
Muni
Nova
Anakhan
Lumino
Luvy
Brighty
Prima
Cheery
Free Joy
Kadula

AND:
Azure
Tutu
Ping Ping
Mei Mei
Prajna
Mirabeau
Laguna
Rainbow
Sunny
Libra

With all my love
In this life and beyond.

Home Photographs by

Supreme Master Ching Hai

Steven André

T. June

Vian Hang

Words from a Child

These are the examples of what should be
The life of our friends, sweet animals.
Be it on land, on air or in the sea.
They should be loved, protected and cherished,
Just like the life that we so wish.

Dearest Heaven, Dear Lord of Karma
Please do love and care for all creatures
For it breaks my heart to see their plight.
I cannot bear to see them suffer.

There're plenty places in Heaven above
Take them all up, and give them love.
This's my little prayer for all beings:

Just your little Love and Compassion.
May all be well, live and let live.
All Love, all care and all forgive.

~ Supreme Master Ching Hai

A Love Song
By Laguna, a Much-loved Macaw
Representing all the winged children in the Supreme Master's household
~ Compiled by Jane

People call Her Supreme Master Ching Hai
Because She comes from the Most High.
But She is our loving Mom
We winged children know Her by.

Her hair is like golden feathers,
Her voice chimes like a bird's.
When She sings us lullabies,
The music lifts us to the highest heavenly worlds.

She comes from a place full of light,
And She brings it to earth for our great delight.
Our house is full of love,
Lots of laughter, good food and sunshine from above.

She is the colors of the rainbow,
The fragrance of a flower.
She is the blessing rain,
The softness of the summer hour.

She is the universe we know so well,
Resting in Her bosom we will never fall.
How can we leave east, west, north and south?
She is them all!

And She is our Mom, above all!!!

Biography of The Supreme Master Ching Hai

The Supreme Master Ching Hai was born in Central Au Lac (Vietnam). At the age of eighteen, Master Ching Hai moved to England to study, and then later to France and then Germany, where She worked for the Red Cross and married a German physician. After two years of happy marriage, with Her husband's blessings, She left Her marriage in pursuit of enlightenment, thus fulfilling an ideal that had been with Her since Her childhood. This began a time of arduous pilgrimages to many different countries that ended only when She met a perfect living Master in the Himalayas. Master Ching Hai received the divine transmission of the inner Light and Sound, which She later called the Quan Yin Method. After a period of diligent practice, She attained Perfect Enlightenment.

To satisfy the longing of sincere Truth seekers, the Supreme Master Ching Hai offers the Quan Yin Method of meditation to people of all nationalities, religions and cultural backgrounds. Her message of love and peace brings spiritual liberation and hope to people throughout the world, reminding all to uphold Truth, Virtue, and Beauty in life.

Contents

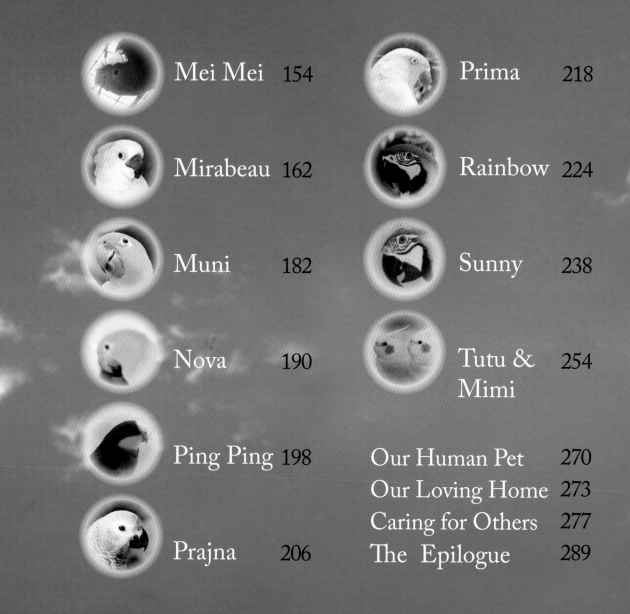

In speaking of God or the Supreme Spirit, Master instructs us to use original non-sexist terms to avoid the argument about whether God is a She or a He.
She + He = Hes (as in Bless)
Her + Him = Hirm (as in Firm)
Hers + His = Hiers (as in Dear)
Example: When God wishes, Hes makes things happen according to Hiers will to suit Hirmself.

As a creator of artistic designs as well as a spiritual teacher, Supreme Master Ching Hai loves all expressions of inner beauty. It is for this reason that She refers to Vietnam as "Au Lac" and Taiwan as "Formosa." Au Lac is the ancient name of Vietnam and means "happiness." And the name Formosa, meaning "beautiful," reflects more completely the beauty of the island and its people. Master feels that using these names brings spiritual elevation and luck to the land and its inhabitants.

Amigo

Paired with Prima, left wild for breeding purpose only. In the beginning, was reserved, nervous, avoided humans…

Later he became more tame and friendly, the better, friendlier of the two.

He gets on well with all the flock, and loves me dearly, bless him so!

Very protective, shoos Prima away if she shows aggression to humans. Before coming here, he was different, and even in the beginning still was afraid of Prima.

As he feels protective to humans, he grew more mature, confident and courageous.

And so lovely.

I am a man
Treat me like one!
For I too am from God
Everyone knows that.

What have I done wrong?
Won't you look at me once?

I feel better among the flowers
Than with that quarrelsome one.
She's beautiful but too strong!

I don't really enjoy being alone
But girls are too hard to get and troublesome
I'll just go meditate on THE ONE

Well! She seems to be friendly
At least she starts talking to me.
I must thank Mother Fairy!

Whatever happens, doesn't matter
I always love a friend like her
She reminds me of the Heavenly Mother

Anakhan

Anakhan means peaceful warrior, I named him thus for his noble manner. He never revenges! Even if he is harassed or injured by another bird.

When Free Joy (Caique) just arrived (the adopted family did not want him because Free Joy is aggressive!) he was attacking Anakhan, twice bit him on the legs, bleeding. We had to take him to the vet, but Anakhan forgave Free Joy always.

Several times Free Joy attacked him again, but Anakhan just wrestled Free Joy upside down on to the ground, placed his foot gently on the Caique's chest for a few seconds, while yelling at him, then let him go, unharmed!

We're amazed at Anakhan's noble demeanor but keep him safe from Free Joy since. For they both would not change their attitude.

I call them War and Peace or Yin and Yang! But strange! They both love me equally intense!

I might look scary
But I am no witchy

I am all loving sweet
All dovey sugar honey!

She is a green palm
I am a black palm

We are both good good

We never do harm
We're from luving realms

Do I want to speak
The complicado human language?
Of course my dear, I do I do!
But would you want to learn
To fly with me too?

I like it much here
See our tops are similar.
When the wind ablowing
Both our "feathers"
Aflying!

Quoa – Quoa!
Mia – Mi – A!
Flo – Rii – Da!

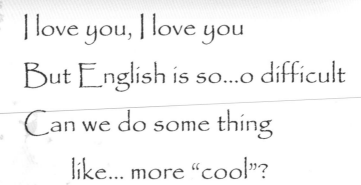

I love you, I love you

But English is so...o difficult

Can we do some thing

like... more "cool"?

Can we use Quan-Yin language?

Which is more universal.

And chic!

A, B, C
    D, E, F, G...
Ah, nothing is more "easy"!
My mom taught me how to fly
But she mentioned none of these!
We just use telepathy.

Azure

Azure, girl of the sky, the color of soft space.

Loves me alone. Absolutely!

She could kiss me the whole day if let her.

For all her love for me, she wards off potential "rivals" zealously. None of the other similar sizes should venture near where she is!

But she's getting more mellowed with age! Good thing! For her petite size, she consumes lots of food! Can eat any thing, any time. One can observe her "stomach" round up like an egg below her throat.

She needs all the calories she can get to keep her body warm, as her belly is bared. One time long ago, I had to leave suddenly and due to regulation, could not bring her with me, nor could I return quickly to the place where she was. Out of sadness she plucked her feathers, and they didn't grow back.

Well! Finally, we are reunited, but she doesn't seem to want those feathers to regrow; she plucks them as soon as they appear, maybe to remind me never to leave her again! I am so sorry, love! You know how my life is, don't you?!!

I, Azure the beauty
Accept your bouquet and apology!

I love you too much
To ever hold a grudge.

No need for your jealousy
Dear Silly Primi!
It will only make you
Less pretty.

In Heaven above
And Earth below
I love only one
You know!

Ok! Ok!
Love is to share:
I'll be patient
And bear!

45

I am always pretty with…

God is the secret of my beauty!

…Or without jewelry You all agree?!!

46

I keep myself in good shape
By certain postures of the yogis.

I think of God
And meditate daily
You see!

I love to be alone

In Nature

Fresh air

On the tree

Smelling nice flowers
Enjoying gifts of the Creator
Singing praises to HER!

One is never alone anyway:
There're always flowers and trees,
And sun, and moon, and stars for company!

And above all: her love,
My human friend's loyalty.
The "real face of yesterday"…

I love you too
I love you three
I love you true...
I love you really~

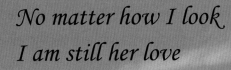

No matter how I look
I am still her love

She doesn't see outer glory
She sees the face of eternity.

Brighty

One day, I thought Luvy was a little lonely among those tiny birdies, so I took him for an outing.

We went shopping together in different pets shop for toys, food etc…

There were different pets and birds in those shops. Luvy paid no attention till he saw Brighty in a small cage. He immediately flew over from my hand, fluttering and climbing around her cage, talking and singing.

So I thought: This is it. Home she came with us. She was rather reserved and shy. Later I found out through the vet that she was sick, and I got a share of that as well. Anyway, we both recovered, quickly. Luvy and Brighty became fast friends ever since.

But she's kind of a not too happy bird. So I named her Brighty, wishing her the better mood. And she changed, became more chattering, more enthusiastic and lively day by day. Thanks Heaven for that…

But she is also nicknamed "Cool beauty" for her distant nature. Luvy on the contrary, has a healthy attitude, is friendly and loving.

It's interesting to see, two almost identical birds of the same species behaving so differently, almost opposite of each other!

Who said like attracts like
Some say opposites attract too!

I feel Brightier

Here on the tree branch

Than in a closed cage

Though it's big and golden!

We mostly go in just to sleep

Thanks Heaven!

Can you GUESS
Whose pictures are these?

Me

(Right! The left is me)

Luvy

Ah! You're so Brighty!
Reward yourself
With the same birdie

61

Difference in
these pictures?

Me
neither!

Nature, Nature
I love you!

I can sing, dance
The whole day through.

(Try it yourself
It's good for you!)

Cheery

Cheery is a hawkhead, so called for the resemblance
of the head of a hawk!

She was "too old" for sale, like some of my other birds.
If not sold at certain age, they are doomed to spend
the rest of their lives in tiny cages, just to make a shop
look like plenty.

She was with another, they befriended each other till
he was sold, left her behind, mourning for love lost.
Heart broken!

I named her Cheery in the hope of cheering her up. She got better each day with TLC. She loves to lie on her back and let you play around, tickling her wings, scratching her tummy…

She didn't want to eat much, so I coaxed her with songs and spoon feeding.

Her mood lifted after some time. Time heals all wounds, they say!

She loves to "help me" clean up the dried leaves from the trees by chewing them off. Feeling proud doing her job every time!

I Love you so much!

God loves you!

Now, upsi-upsi once more time
Make you *beautiful*, **strong** and *wise!*

❤ One for Momy

❤ One for Dady

❤ One more for you

❤ And one for me!

We feel good, we feel fine.

We feel rested after a good nite!

And meditation is really... nice.

Good morning Ma'am, Good morning sun.

Thanks for breakfast and loving concern!

I love God for every bit of nutrient

Now let's go work and prune the trees
And anything that makes you pleased

"Bravo, bravo, well done, well done
You're a good girl! And diligent!"

And now just for the two of us

Love, love, love, more love and trust.

You meditate for both of us
I gotta finish working this nut!

Well, have you been in Nirvana
Would you like nut from Samsara!

(*)Note: Nirvana = Heaven
Samsara = Earth

Free Joy

"Thou shalt not love any other bird beside me"

Free Joy was another unwanted bird. Too old to be sold. If a bird stays too long alone, he/she will find it difficult to get along with other birds or a mate.

Free Joy was an "angry-youngster" and distrusted men. But he adores women, and he loves me absolute! I can do anything with him, while he might bite any near comer male with no fear or reservation! Size never matters to him.

He loves doing acrobatics on my finger, turning himself 360° around it. He is ever so gentle with ladies.

He can hop and dance on command like a circus talent! He sings well too, and is a free spirit.

Originally I offered him as a partner to a lonely female Caique in a vet clinic. But he wanted nothing to do with her. So the vet returned him to me.

The moment he is on my hand and out of the vet's place, he let out a string of songs like pearls and waterfall; he was ecstatic with joy and showed a full tank of happiness.

I named him Free Joy on the spot. It's just so right for him. And he lives up to this name always. You never see a dull moment in him!

Such a darling of my heart; full of love for life and joy to live!

Thank You God
Thank You Heaven!

For Free Joy's first day home!
What a joy… and fun!
We all feel this's where he belongs!

Acrobic tat, acrobat tic

Upside down, inside out, I am blissed!

As long as I am with you

There's nothing I wouldn't do!

Am I happy? Of course I am

I am smiling, I am singing

I can also hop and I can dance

Just to show you how happy I am

(God would tell you the same!)

I never felt so good before

There, there you are!

I could do much more!

See the difference between fotos?

This one has leaves on it.

And on this one: no!

I ate them all!

(Just to see Heaven better)

Life is joyful, life is free

Life is cool like a coco tree!

A big thanks to Mommy,

And God Almighty!

I love THEE!

Gentino

Gentino is a Molucan cockatoo, the type of bird that is associated with loyalty and lifetime devotion to the human companion.

I got to know him when he was already 20 years old. But he's ever energetic and young! He talks to you, to himself, he sings, he dances.

He was a little sad when the "ex" handed him over to me, but quickly got over it and came to love me dearly. As he knows he's not wanted anymore!

When I brought him back to his previous "owner," he shied away from him and ran back into my arms, snuggled his head onto my bosom, showing affection to me more than ever before that day!

Whenever my car comes home, no matter how late, he is the first one to say, "Hallo," "How are you," "I love you," "Come here."

One time when he misbehaved, I reprimanded him seriously, he looked down to the floor and said, "I am sorry" clearly! But that's the only time he said it.

He loves to be in my company and ignores other birds. But he loves dogs. He loves to preen and groom them, especially the long-haired ones. He will chase after them, cooing, "Come here, wou wou, good boy, good boy"… and the dogs are scared of him, even the big dogs like Hermit and Goody. Because he would stand on top of them and "comb" their hair, and of course if they move their hair gets pulled. It hurts, I guess. (You can try to see how it feels like!)

Otherwise, he would want to kiss them, and it's not a soft beak that he has!

He also likes to watch the dogs fooling around and say, "Ha ha, it's funny!" (I did not teach him all this.) There is no end to his antics, ever.

He has a very special place in my heart always. Dearest baby love Gentino of mein…

Wow! What a big difference
Is it already Heaven?
    I haven't seen the sky
    For such a long long time
    Quoa! Quoa! Quoa!
    I have a brand new life.

I can see far

to the vast horizon

I could even fly

But I want to stay forever here

Just by her side.

Ah, here she came
My "little angel"
I'd even come down right
From Heaven just to say Hi!
I haven't seen her near
(since last nite!)
I missed her in my dream
I miss her any time!

... Just to think of my ex place

Oh dear Heaven, how I hate!...

I often chewed away boredom

If only can also the cage.

~...~

I was placed at the "bottom line"

Dirt and dirt fly around day and nite

Above my cages other birds scream so loud

Under my cage filth + poo abounds!

EX PLACE

Guess who tries to look alike
But not as handsome as I...?

No, no, no! It is not me
Don't you know I am so pretty?
Even though he came here before
I am top bird, and I am adored!

(Shz! Don't tell this to Mirabeau!)

Look at the dogs I love to preen
But I'll be patient and waiting.
They are my favorite long hair
How adorable even they're just ...
Lying there!

99

See the proof?

That I am so loved!

By the birds and humans alike

I am the "center of this life"!

Ha ha!

(Believe it? Well, try...!)

Why bother with him and Mirabeau

I am right here as if you don't know

If I were you, I'd put them down

And come hurried to me... right now!

There, there, ok that feather there

It bugs me much cos it's so hard

I really love your tender touch

Appreciate your care ever so much

If there's Heaven some where above

I pray God let me be with you, love!

Kadula

Kadula is a beautiful scarlet. So affectionate and sensitive and loyal. I love this girl so much for her heart as much as her beauty.

She is another case of depression through sudden separation! She was together with a male scarlet, then he was sold. Leaving her alone and sad.

But she was trying to adjust while in my house. Then she recovered and showed signs of happiness.

When she first came into my car to go home, she seemed to pick herself up and sing "la la la la" all the way home.

But still, it takes long time for her to be her normal happy self.

I wish we could all understand others like birds, and treat them as we would ourselves… They are so sensitive in their emotional relationships, and in the atmosphere they are surrounded with.

Their companion and friends mean a lot to them, sometimes as life itself, their loyalty is so incredible! They suffer loss and sorrow much like we do.

All who have birds should consider their feeling and have respect for their dignity and love.

"before"

This is the me "before"
I looked even more miserable

I look better here already
And feel better day by day

(not long)

"after"

Life will improve someway, surely
I did not know that I could try
Here I have love and company
That lifts me out of misery!

Thank You my Lord!

You are so gracious.

You heard my prayers

I love You forever!

This new lady friend really loves birds

Went out of her way to bring us pleasure

She builds all kinds in her garden

To make us feel like in Heaven

She gives good food and lots of toys

And natural home for us to enjoy

And so of course I get better

As you can see, I recover!

Because of such a love and care

That in this world I think so rare

I am grateful, that's all I can share.

I love this guy he is so cute

With sunny mood and bell-like "drills."

He dances, he sings, and makes merry

And he looks so gorgeous to me.

(I think he's trying to please... somebody!)

Tell me Sunny, is that somebody, me?

I also like you so...o a lot...lot

After – you know – the Lord our God

And I really

love this lady

Even if no one exists in this world

She will always be there for me!

Laguna

Named for her beautiful color of mysterious deep water.

But she is anything but mysterious. She plays with humans (not all) laughs and talks a lot. She is like an open book. If she's not pleased, you can't get her out onto your hand. If she's happy she lies on her back at the bottom of the cage, playing with her tail, singing all the while! And she knows who is who!

She makes big conversation, which sounds like human (learnt from television). Now and again you can make out some words: "OK, now get over it, I don't like you, well how are you, I love you, Laguna, Laguna… where are you going," etc.

She amuses herself a lot and is no trouble. Except if she gets to the top of her cage. She doesn't want to come down!

She'll push anything (and you) away with her beak and run around goose chase with you; only new, colorful food can lure her back in, after a considerable long time playing hard to get.

But she loves and respects me so much; she even told one bird communicator that I'm a very special lady, should be highly revered!

She also loves to cuddle in my arm or lie on her back so I stroke her belly. She can eat up any cage that is not as thick as the size of a metal stick you use for BBQ. She can even twist them around into a tight spiral shape, wrapped around the other edge of the cage like a lock, that pliers must be used to open the door to get her out or for feeding, cleaning. Those metal wires are thick enough for you to find it not easy to cut through with metal cutters. But she can break them with her beak!!!

It's good that she's friendly with humans and other pets! She loves all nuts, and is addicted to melon, apples and mango. She chews wood like you chew bread. Such a strong jaw, and strong personality.

But I adore her and she loves me.

Hallo big green gate

That I always hate!

　　You can't separate me

　　And the one I love dearly

　　I'd climb mountains and rivers

　　Just to be near her!

If we are together

Me no fear blizzard thunder!

Above I have God

Here... her.

I miss you too

I love you too

I'll just stay right here

I won't move!

120

Well, maybe away a little
Like here, just around the corner
To hear what the trees say
About true love every day.

Love is all we need

We show it with kiss...!

This funny thing I don't like

Why, it is blocking your eyes!

I wana see your love

I wana see your light...

Do you really know who am I?

The one who came from the Light

125

And do you know who you are?

The one from galaxies afar

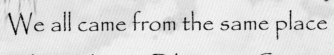

We all came from the same place
That is Love, Blessing, Grace!

(To animal –psychic:)

And you know who's this woman?

She is "Love – incarnation."

Libra

A Hybrid macaw, his temperament is also "Hy Brid." Sometimes he's sweet, other times a little tough. But deep down he's a "Good Boy."

I named him Libra to "balance" him.

When he first came, also a little too old to sell, but he adjusted well. He kissed me the first time home(!!!)

He loves to buddy with everyone. But he comes on too strong, so they detour themselves away from him.

Only Sunny stayed on. Being a good natured, happy go lucky whatever type, Sunny gets on with everyone. Live and let live alike.

So they became fast friends, and Libra adores Sunny and thus settled down with the flock quickly.

Despite his rough style, he is very good at heart, sentimental and sensitive.

One day I had to leave, not knowing when I will ever return nor whether I will be able to bring them to me later. I wasn't even sure where I will be. So I went to each of them tearfully saying good-bye. Telling them how sorry I am to leave suddenly this way.

Libra, normally cool and not showing emotion, suddenly grabbed me before I even reached his cage and tilted his head on my arm when I came next to him, "kiss kiss" me gently, rubbing his head on to me, then looked up into my eyes "saying" it's OK, it's going to be OK. I love you. I will miss you. But don't worry, you will see us again.

Well, that made me cry more like a baby! So much love I felt from that tough but small frame of a wonder being!

I thanked Heaven for such a marvel of creation and feel so privileged to understand someone who is not human, but who is so beautiful inside out.

If you have pets, try to "listen"; they will lead you into their world, guarded secretly since the beginning of creation!

Hi there world! Nice to be here.

I have naught to loose nor to fear

Where I came from I was alone

It's a good thing: to learn detachment.

I like her cos she's genuine
She's unconditional and loving.

She let me be and I'm happy
Besides, I love being among trees
Like Buddha under the Bodhi.

I have good food, lots of toys and love
Lots of play time and such stuff
If Nirvana means without desire
Then it is here right by my side

I offer my thanks to Heaven up there
For my little life extraordinaire
To be a pet and enjoy all this
All day, all nite I am in bliss!

And thanks to this lovely lady
You are in my heart through eternity
I offer my "hand" in lasting friendship
My love, I am all yours to keep!

Hip Hip!

A quiet moment on God above

My heart has never lacked Hiers love

I meditate on Hiers blessing

Forever showers on all beings

Lumino

I don't know if any bird could ask for more colors than Lumino, an Eastern Rosella, beloved of my heart.

And when he sings, Heaven would be also pleased. He created so many beautiful tunes to match his even glorious appearance! He is an incredible musician, such a tiny being with so much life and vigor.

He is also a loner, shy and reserved. Maybe all artists are in someway. But you can be allowed to feel his love, once he gets to know you well enough.

He doesn't give his heart just to any one; he chooses discretely, and stays with his choice and shows his affection in a quiet but lovely way. Thus, when he perched on my shoulder for the first time, and let me take him out of his "room," there was a tingling sensation under my skin!

There's no way you can miss this feeling of affection and oneness. I love him so much, no words can describe. And his love cannot be compared or measured. How such a fragile frame holds so much splendor!

I shall forever cherish you, treasured gift of my life, dearest beloved Lumino. Your love brings tears of gratitude to my eyes.

And maybe to anyone, who has the privilege to know it.

Just to say hallo,

And I do love you so.

I am not hungry

Do not worry

Thanks for the nice surrounding

In which I am thriving.

The only important things in these pictures
Are "me and her"

The rest?
Well, no matter!

All the branches

I did not chew!

Who has thus told you?

I was just checking them through

The photographer

Wants me to show all colors.

Here you have it.

Voilà!

I say so long

But not good-bye

You stay forever

In this heart of mine

We live together

In the eternal life!

Luvy

Luvy, so named for his soft, tender loving nature.

He is so totally into you, that he makes you feel that you are the only person in his entire life's focus. He talks clearly and sweetly, with a throatal low voice that's so cute.

Though he loves Brighty so much, I'm still the priority; he shows it well! He never complains, always bears a bright, happy and positive attitude, so he helped Brighty recover from her depression, and cheers my day. Just his devotional love is even enough for anyone to feel warmed up and happy.

He came from a high level of consciousness. He brought with him this loving unconditional gift into the human world. We are lucky to have our planet populated with these special of special beings who brighten our world with their beauty and true love.

He always says to me: "I love you." And gives me kisses, and shows his joy and appreciation even just for any little nice gesture or food. Of course he loves peanuts!

One day while he was in a covered terrace, somehow he landed on the floor, and separated by a curtain, he couldn't get out. But he stayed there and talk to himself, as if to keep calm while the wind kept beating the curtain against his head, till I heard and found him!

Then he clung to my finger desperately, and said non-stop: "I love you, I love you, I love you".....

I placed him onto my chest and caressed him, he became still and drifted into his dream soon after.

He's such a sweet darling that leaves a deep loving impression on anyone who knows him. God bless him so.

And I can't even begin to express how much he means to me and how much I love this marvel of a creature!

There you have it

I'm all smile and "photo-chic"!

If you like my pose alright.

Make my photo smart and bright.

'Course I can sing, loud and clear

I have come into this world to cheer

If you feel a little low and down

I will sing you up to the high cloud!

We say halo, never good-bye

For we are eternal Light

Even if our physical disappears

Our real essence is always here.

Mei Mei

Mei Mei – Chinese, meaning beautiful sister, so named for her maiden- like personality. This bird, together with Ping Ping are new family members.

Like Prima and Amigo, they were left wild in an outdoor cage for breeding purpose only.

I took them in because of some affinity in the past.

They have code words to be recognized. Hers is "smart bird"; I used that to tame her, and she became more accepting and happy.

Tell her that she is a "smart bird" - then you can see her spirit spark up, her attitude cheer on and she'll come to you on offered perch, or get back into her cage effortlessly.

But it took long time for this pair to be tamed, in the beginning, as they're so used to being in the "wild outdoors." They were so fearful of humans that we couldn't even come near; they would either panic or bite if too close.

They do not bite anymore! And I came in and out in the night to check their room's temperature "un-noticed."

She is a very keen observer and not much escapes her sharp eyes. So she knows who's with her and who's not, who she can trust and who to stay distanced from. You can feel her watching eyes even from behind you or from a far corner of the room. But it's not an uncomfortable feeling, just OK, un-intrusive.

And though remaining cool, she sends you love, affection in the air. And you feel that with her appreciation for your care and sincerity. (If you have!)

I love outdoors, I love fresh air
I love the wind caressing my hair
Climbing the tree is my fav. sport
Singing in the sun is another lot.

157

I am not afraid of any height

Here you can see me hanging upside

I want to see the blue Heaven

That – my original nature – reminds

I love water, I love shower
I dip myself any time.
"Cleanliness is close to Godliness":
I want to remember Him always.

Mirabeau

My first bird ever since "adulthood." I had a black bird before as a child, but I set him free as he was captured in the wild and given to me untamed. I thus didn't want to cage him.

Originally he was named Mirabele, as the previous caretaker told me it's a female – but a DNA test later showed that he was a male – so I changed his name to Mirabeau.

Well, it doesn't matter. He is as lovely as a female and as loyal as a dog. No matter how many birds came after, he always shows me the same affection as the first time we met. Even more so!

Anytime or no matter how late I come in, he always runs to the door for a loving cuddle.

He was very young when I came across him, he is my "official" first chosen bird. Or maybe he chose me.

When I came in, he started to greet me and cuddled right away. Then he quietly lay down on a table as if asleep. I felt we were very connected, but my mind was unsure whether or not to bind myself with responsibility.

I asked him half jokingly: "Are you ready to go home?" And to everyone's surprise, amid the talk of humans, birds, dogs and pets of all kind, the sleeping baby bird stood up and walked straight toward me among the crowd, stepped on my hand, laid his head on my bosom, looked at me lovingly and knowingly in a definite "Yes" in front of everyone.

So I "had to" take him home! And we live happily ever after since. Well, sometimes we had "words," but no big trouble. Just like on some occasion when he cut off my TV program by chewing away the live electric cord. (Well, TV is not always good for you!) Or, he demolished my furniture. (OK, renunciation is better!) Or, he ate up my shirt button. (Yogis don't need clothes anyway.) I just have to watch him; if let alone anything in the house can be his "object of demolition"; he doesn't chew on toys that much, just loves to chew forbidden things!

One day, in some moment, we were busy, he got to the ceiling at the entrance door frame, munched all the cable for the awning system and sat up there in the middle of messy gnawed zigzag wires, waiting for me to come take him down (and scold him of course!)

Despite all his troublesome antics, I always kiss him good-nite, for his love is worth all the possessions in the world.

Guess which bird I like the best?
Well, the middle one, and the rest.

I'll try to bring it right down
Who would ever need a gate.
She's not home and she is late,
This is the one doth us separate!

Wonder why I transmigrate here
But I love being among these peers
They're all colors and each own size
And we get along fabulously fine!

Hi there housy, I am taller than you
Think that you can contain me, noo!
I am not the body I inhabit,
I am one with the vast spirit!
You and I
How we forget sometimes.

I KNOW YOU LIKE ME, MIRABEAU
BUT AIN'T I TOO BIG FOR YOU?

OH, IT DEPENDS ON HOW YOU LIVE
ALL THINGS ON EARTH ARE RELATIVE!

WHAT'S GREAT IS THE REAL ONE WITHIN NO SIZE, NO DEATH, NO BIRTH, EVERLASTING.

That secret of the universe
Not everyone understood.
Methinks!

I am a bird who dreams
Or in a dream become a bird!

But I don't mind this illusion
Which is as sweet as in Heaven!

It's OK to be alone
One can contemplate on the "unknown"

But I also love to be
With my saintly family.

And of course

I love this lady.

Muni

One of the more affectionate queens of Bavaria, he is actually a male.

So lovely, lovely. You can do anything you want with him: turn him "inside out" upside down, he just loves it. He loves to be scratched gently on his tumtum (tummy).

Anything you do, he'd approve and always says: "Correct. Correct. Correct!"

He comes to the door of his "condo," waiting to be taken out if I am near. The two of them are much affectionate about each others, always showing love, always grooming each other, inseparable. Well, no wonder: they are brother and sister!

But they look like twins; you can only tell the difference as Nova (the other) has more green feathers on the back of her shoulder.

He is so affectionate, you'd like to spend all day playing with him!

I am definitely not a queen here.
The title makes me feel a little "Queer."
Can assure you I'm 100% macho
I am just too young to show!

We are quite different though we look like twins.
The one behind me is the real queen.
But she is real sweet and not snobbish!
For the true royal is the mighty spirit.
We came from there and will be back soon.
Beyond the stars, the suns and moons.

186

Yeah! I could lie here day and nite.
As long as you're holding me tight
What treasure I on earth the most?
Everyone knows: it is your Love!

Yeah! Turn me round, turn upside down
As long as you're here, no matter how

Like this I see more of Heaven
And feel your love equal to none.

Nova

Nova, I only want to say I love you so much, and you know it's true. God bless you.

My beautiful much loved queen

My pure - hearted heavenly being

Though this world is not really fit for you

To show your love, you have come down.

The human race considered blessed

That God sends them, among the best

You gift this world with your beauty

But leave sadness when you've gone away!

I love you Nova, for as long as I live

And forever, forever more.

Beyond this illusionary dream

We will stay lasting friends.

I don't have any jealousy.
You love me as much as Muni.
But he's a boy and I'm a girl.
Tell me which one you prefer?
(Just kidding!)

It is interesting to see
The world in "Topsy Turvy."
But I like much this position
Having higher, clearer "viewpoint."

And… So I can see your whole face
And… So much feel the Heaven's Grace
The world is beautiful when we're together.
Deep in my heart, I thank the Creator.

Me and Muni
Love you dearly
We think of you
Day and Nite through.
We love you!

Ping Ping

Together with Mei Mei, they were left wild
but in small cage. Of course just for breeding.
However, they'd not hesitate to separate them
if profited. So I took them both.

His code is "Pretty Bird" as he is proud of his splendor. Who wouldn't be? I just use this code to train him. So he'd go on my hand and tame him.

But for this, one needs lots of patience, time and love. As they both have been wild. Whenever you stop "interacting" with them even for a short while due to lack of time, they'd go back to the untamed state.

But it's OK anyway; in my house, each one is free to choose the intimacy between us. It's alright also, just to enjoy each other's presence, and have their needs taken cared of. They have each other anyway. And we do love and trust each other as a family. They're both OK with that. Me too.

The most important point is that we are all happy. And we are.

As God is my witness

Here, I am the prettiest

Hes's made me so

To adorn this world

I am doing my noble duty

Just to... BE!

Thanks Heaven that we're so lucky

That we are together every day

That we have a nice home, caring love

We also thank our kind lady

For protecting and loving us

We love each other

We also love her.

I love to fly around trees high

My heart feels as vast as the sky

There's nothing can contain my spirit

For within me Heaven's might is!

The view is lovely, like you're, Mei Mei

Our dear FATHER creates beauty

Our dear MOTHER creates true love

It is Heaven everywhere I see!

Prajna

She came to me as a "baby." A doctor for birds recommanded me to take her home. Well, I did.

I spoon-fed her till she was weaned. She loves to be scratched on her head ever since she came home, even now. No matter how late I come in (to check the birds' room temperature, make sure it's cool/warm enough for them at night), she always comes near to greet me and bow down her head.

I always sing softly before and upon entering their room with a small flashlight shining on my face, so that they'd not be alarmed. And she also sings with me.

Or she'll say, "Yoo hoo," cos I do that sometimes. And she clicks her tongue also the way I do, then comes near for the head "pet pet."

She is so adorable and she keeps Mirabeau quiet. Before when Mirabeau was alone, he would yell a lot more often and louder. He's happier with her company. They get along well.

She talks exactly like my voice – sometimes fools the assistants, thinking that I am nearby! If I tell my helpers something, and they don't respond, she'll say "Yes Master" – for their sake!

She would call any dog's name with precision. Like "Benny, quiet" "Hermit, no" etc… When the dogs are too loud! And of course, "I love You" when she feels like it if I am near (with a peanut!).

I am big girl: grow in God's love
Who needs spoon feeding stuff
(As if I am still a baby!)
All the mothers! The same worry!

The flowers and I
Who is prettier?
I can't stop
Feeling the wonders.
God Almighty must be very wise
To create beauties like you and I

And Hes also created this girl
So she can love and care for birds
I don't know which planet she's from
But what would I do without her!

I look around and around me
Beauty and love everywhere I see

I thank Heaven and God above
For all the care and all the Love

213

In this dream land of temporal
Of illusion and upheaval
The love of God will see me through....

And I love life.
Because of Y♥u!

Summer, winter is all the same
'Cause in my home I'm always warm.

They say I came from Africa
(No! From the "House of my FATHER")
— said my Master! —

And I believe her!

Prima

She is just beautiful.

She is just … Prima.

And she likes to stay atop.

> You cannot buy her
>
> You cannot charm her
>
> Unless you are dark-colored
>
> At least dark-haired
>
> And a male
>
> A human male.

She would not change for any reason. That's how she is. And I accept it. It's OK. But we are friends. And she would let me ferry her around on my shoulder – alone – She'd nip my ear if some "other" is sharing my trip!

And she can be loud for such a small size of a bird. You can hear her through tight doubled glaze windows, closed doors. Sound proof glass…

She can be friendly if she wants a peanut, a piece of apple or free ride: she'd come near to me and say: "Prima want to go out" and repeating it till I "understand" that she means business or else! (quack loud, bite the locks, kick the cage etc…)

But I love her so much so…so…so… much. I'd like to hug her close and say that now--God bless her soul!

I don't mind being alone
Especially in the wide open.
My dear God loves me to be free
Among pretty flower and shady trees.
(~said my lady~)

(Azure) Let me make it clear to you
He is Mein!...
And she is too!

But we'll share the same Heaven
I let you, 'cause you're my friend!

OK, Amigo!
I declare hereby to forgive you
"As you forgive your transgressor
God in Heaven will forgive you..."

Don't ever again be so close to... that blue!

Rainbow

Rainbow is the most "Psychic" of all my birds. He conveys many things to me for which I am amazed and grateful. He is the more of a "Go between" to let me know certain things about the flock, and other useful revelations.

He is generally very gentle, and does not fight back at any provocation. But you can tell if he's upset, though he's so patient and has great endurance. He's very protective of Laguna, the two are good friends. They groom each other lovingly, kiss and regurgitate to share food (a bird's sure sign of affection).

If left alone, he would often open (numbered) locks to come out of his cage to be near Laguna.

And no matter how big the cage is, he'll stick close to her in some corner.

I call him also "Hanger" 'cause he loves to hang at the top of the cage by hooking all his claws onto the metal ceiling fence, even to sleep. And he even managed to convince Laguna to do the same whenever they're together.

Alone, she would seldom do that by herself. If Sunny is with Rainbow, he will also hang himself in the air like him.

Rainbow is a very affectionate bird, but could get jealous if with Laguna. Well, I guess that happens also in the (hu)man world!

I love climbing, anywhere will do
I'd climb Heaven if I could too.

— ✮ —

Where I came from we are hangers
We hang on to love forever.
Hang on to God, virtue, beauty
To the nobleness that we should be.

Don't ask for the impossible
Why, first comes first perches, no?!
Though I love you so dearly
Stay down there till I'm ready!

Laguna might have given up.
But not I, Rainbow at the top.

Did I change my mind?
— well, gentlemen do sometimes!
It's nice to be nice.

This one sure make me more like me.

We birds do like good quality.

We like respect
  And we like love

Without those things what will life be?

I didn't like this picture,
So told him take another.

And we do love our dear "Birdies"
That "Sunny" is really funny
When asked by Mom if he's happy
He answers: Ni Hao? In Chinesy: (How're you?)

When asked by others, "How are you?"
He said, "Ha Ha"!
So we all laugh: Quoa, Quoa, Quoa!

*"Please say something
Loved Rainbow"!*

*Come hang with me
... If you are bored!*

233

This is as luv as it can get.

She does anything to make me happy.

I'll do anything to make her pleased.

Ha ha hi hi!

In her arms, I'm a baby!

I ask nothing more from God,
Such gratefulness has filled my heart!

Such happiness, such contentment
Makes me blissful as in Heaven.
Thanks God for giving me her Love.
And wonderful meditation!

Sunny

One fine afternoon, I walked into a pet shop with Mirabeau on my shoulder, looking for a "play tree" and some new toys for him.

The sales woman in the shop showed me the best she had in the shop – A sturdy big hard wood "tree" with swing, ring and lots of branches to run around. I purchased all I needed there and I went to pay. While there, the same sales woman asked me if I

take my bird everywhere
I go, and if this expensive
play tree and toys were for him. I
answered, "Yes."

She commented what a lucky bird he is, then
asked me whether I wanted to adopt her
macaw blue and gold. He was 11 months
old then and very sweet tempered (Well,
at that tender age!!!)She had him since his
babyhood. I was surprised that someone
would "give away" her own bird, asking for a
price with cage included! (A reasonable price
you could get one brand new for both.)

I wanted to know why. She explained the
lack of time and attention for him. Hence he's
showing sign of stress; plucking his feathers,
looking unhappy and so on… And she saw
me take so much care for Mirabeau, thinking
he'll be better with me.

So I drove to her home, paid the price, got the sales paper, and took him with me. I felt so sorry for Sunny that no one asked his opinion and nor considered his feeling.

For the next two weeks, he was in bad shape, crying a lot, didn't want to eat much. At the time I already bought a big cage for Sunny (renamed thus to cheer up his life, cut off connection with the sad past). But I thought maybe his small old cage would be more familiar to him and make him feel more at home.

So I sent my assistant to go pick up that old, narrow rusty cage, hoping to make Sunny feel better, it didn't. He kept screaming, crying for "Dad, Dad." Obviously that's what he learnt to call the ex male "owner" who took more care of him than his wife -- I still want to cry now, thinking of what he must have gone through!

One day I told him after so much effort of trying to console him without success: "Stop it! That family didn't want you. That's why you are here." – At this remark, he cried heartbrokenly, I was so sorry, I cried so much too, and apologized profusedly.

"I am sorry, I'm sorry, I didn't mean to hurt you, I love you so much, please settle down. We all love you here, and I will take care of you for the rest of your life, with all the love and care you need." And I touched his cage, kept talking, and then he calmed down and we both sat there quietly, only my true love for him communicating from my heart.

He healed soon after, and became more enthusiastic about life around him. He said,

"I like apple" if I asked. He loves mango more, and Banana second.

Birds would teach you about their world, their loyalty, their emotional needs, sensitivity and about love. They are so beautiful inside and outside.

They deserve love, TLC and respect, and show appreciation if you care — I have never regretted having brought any of my birds home. They give unconditional love, adorn my face with smiles and brighten my daily coexistence with the world.

They bridge the gap between human and other creatures. I only want to make them happy in my home, as members of my family.

I love my name
Sunny I am
I live in God's Light
I feel so sunshine.

We look so much alike
Good Rainbow and I
Only Mom could tell us apart
For others it may be hard.

Let me check out your hand glove
See if the stuff is good enough
I'll be so "gento."
Won't hurt your "fingos."

Yesterday you were blue
Today you are red.
What kind of feather
is that?

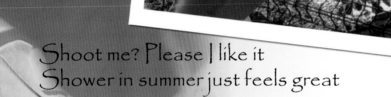

Shoot me? Please I like it
Shower in summer just feels great

Over the back and under wings
It's so co...ol and re...freshi...ing.

It's me Sunny, not Rainbow
A while ago, I let him borrow
Well, we share everything together
In our home, there is no owner
God gives us and on we pass
We don't hoard things that will not last

Just checking out this carpet
See if it's soft on her feet.
She takes good care of us all
A guy should return something, no?

Dearest good and sweet camera
I'd like to say something to ya
That I'm happy, grateful, content
Thanks to m'lady and grace of Heaven
Tell everyone I'm a lucky bird
Have found the "home of love" forever.

The sky is not the limit?

People say the sky is the limit
But Mom-Mom said that's not it
"You have to fly beyond the stars
Beyond Milky Ways and constellations afar!"

Woa!

I am sure as you say there is a Heaven
But where'ver you are that's where I'm going.
Because of you I love this EARTH
Because of You I'd forsake the world!

251

Tutu & Mimi

Tutu and Mimi, "Twin" sisters, my first and only cockatiels, lovely beyond words.

When we first encountered each other, they jumped right onto my hands, then perched each on one side of my shoulder – stayed on. That's how they got "carried" into my house.

The two of them together with Mirabeau traveled to many places in my mobile home, enjoyed family vacation style and we had no problem.

They love to perch on shoulder, transported free around or on the back of the sofa, watching TV!

And they love to groom me. Preening my hair, one side each, diligently! Oh, I love them so. I could cry, thinking of their "Little Big" love.

Whenever they hear my voice, no matter at what hour, from anywhere, they chirp very loud, calling me and rushing to greet me excitedly upon my entering. One cannot but feel their love written all over their tiny bodies and springing feet, with loud, high notes of welcoming and joy of reunion.

Oh, I love you so! If humans could love each other that much, peace and happiness can be ours forever.

We are Mimi (left), and Tutu (right)
We are very beautiful and bright
And although we look like twins
Mom can tell who is who in a twinkling

Tell you a little secret:
I'm a little paler
Mimi is a little reddish.

Her temperament too, is!

Though we are such a big family
Mom still so loves Tu and Mimi
She just said that "Love is to share"
We do always with other pairs.

But we sometimes go on solo
Around the garden to explore.
To appreciate God's immense love
Written on each leaf and flower!

Or to sit under the tree like a Buddha

Inspired by His saintly nature

To thank and praise Heaven above

As we can feel and live in God's Love.

Let's groom Mom while she's busy
She should look great if you ask me

I'm over here and you're over there
Preening away her bad feathers.

You can see here we're in the yard
Sharing love, toys and perch together.

When you are close
I enjoy your being

When you're not here
Of you I think

I feel your love all nite and day
Whether you're here or far away.

Going by yourself?

    It's too lonely!

How about Tutu

    Keeps you companied.

Our Human Pet

This's our dear human pet girl
That we the lucky flock adore
Run out of words for affection
We just simply call her "Mom Mom."

Our human pet
Here with one of our favorites

Our Loving Home

So much she loves us
You can see the fuss.

There, she did thus invent
Our new winter play pen!

This is just a sample
Some are much bigger.

She spent many days outdoors
Even February nites also
To finish this product of love
Then proudly presented our condos

We enjoy the view
Without the winter chill.

Caring for Others

She loves them (outside birds)
Because they have wings...

This girl pet is a mystery
Why, she goes and loves everybody!
But we think it's 'cause she loves us too much
So she loves anyone who looks like us…

We also sympathize with the less lucky
The "homeless" birds like these!

A CONVERSATION WITH... GO...OSE?

That's too far!

Well OK! It's a SWA...AN

But... what's the point?

(Besides it's a wild one!!!)

Meaning comes and ...GO...NE!!!

Nothing wrong with comforting the needy
We're proud cos they look like us birdies:
So she loves them for they look similar
And they have wings like us at home here.

...And look similar to us...

Or...(NOT!!!)

Watch it!
They might have ticks!

AND WHAT IS...
THEN... THIS???

Oh God!...

She even loves

The… the flowers!!!

Also they are?…

Family members???

The Epilogue

You are the heavenly angels
Descending onto Earth.

Related Information

For more information about communicating with and caring for our animal friends, along with inspiring stories from Master about Her other special animal companions, please refer to the following videotapes and DVDs.

DVD 712 The Divine Intelligence of Animals
20010605 Florida Center, U.S.A.

#713 Love Is the Master
20010605 Florida Center, U.S.A.

DVD 718 Love Is Always Good
20010607 Florida Center, U.S.A.

DVD 719 Overcoming Bad Habits
20010609 Florida Center, U.S.A.

DVD 721 The Wisdom Eye
20010604 Florida Center, U.S.A.

#724 Sincerity and Purity of Heart
20010612~ 20010616 Florida Center, U.S.A.

#725 A Humble Way of Life
20011222~ 20011223 Florida Center, U.S.A.

DVD 726 A Selfless Motive
20011223 Florida Center, U.S.A.

#730 To Communicate by Love
20011225, 20011226 Florida Center, U.S.A.

#734 The Touch of a Master
20011226~ 20011227 Florida Center, U.S.A.

#735 The Courage To Change
20011228~ 20011230 Florida Center, U.S.A.

#747 Children of the Dragon and Fairy Master's Birthday Celebration 2002
20020511, 20020513 Florida Center, U.S.A.

DVD 780 The Dogs and the Birds in My Life
Dedicated to All Earth's Co-inhabitants

The Noble Wilds

The third book written *by*
Supreme Master Ching Hai

Is coming soon!

The Spiritual Teachings by The Supreme Master Ching Hai

The Key of Immediate Enlightenment

A collection of The Supreme Master Ching Hai's lectures. Available in Aulacese (1-15), Chinese (1-10), English (1-5), French (1-2), Finnish (1), German (1-2), Hungarian (1), Indonesian (1-5), Japanese (1-4), Korean (1-11), Mongolian (1,6), Portuguese (1-2), Polish (1-2), Spanish (1-3), Swedish (1), Thai (1-6), and Tibetan (1).

The Key of Immediate Enlightenment – Questions and Answers

A collection of questions and answers from Master's lectures.
Available in Aulacese (1-4), Bulgarian, Chinese (1-3), Czech, English (1-2), French, German, Hungarian, Indonesian (1-3), Japanese, Korean (1-4), Portuguese, Polish, and Russian.

The Key of Immediate Enlightenment – Special Edition/Seven-Day Retreat

A collection of Master's lectures in1992 during a Seven-Day Retreat in San Di Mun, Formosa. Available in English and Aulacese.

The Key of Immediate Enlightenment – Special Edition/1993 World Lecture Tour

A six-volume collection of The Supreme Master Ching Hai's lectures during the 1993 World Lecture Tour. Available in English and Chinese.

Letters Between Master and Spiritual Practitioners

Available in Aulacese (1-2), Chinese (1-3), English (1), Spanish (1)

The Key of Immediate Enlightenment –My Wondrous Experiences with Master (1-2)

Available in Chinese and Aulacese.

Master Tells Stories

Available in Aulacese, Chinese, English, Japanese, Korean, Spanish, and Thai.

Of God and Humans – Insights from Bible Stories

Available in English and Chinese.

God Takes Care of Everything
Illustrated Tales of Wisdom from The Supreme Master Ching Hai

Aulacese, Chinese, English, French, Japanese, and Korean.

The Supreme Master Ching Hai's Enlightening Humor –
Your Halo Is Too Tight!

Available in Chinese and English.

Coloring Our Lives

A collection of quotes and spiritual teachings by Master. Available in Chinese and English.

Secrets to Effortless Spiritual Practice

Available in Chinese and English.

God's Direct Contact – The Way to Reach Peace

A collection of The Supreme Master Ching Hai's lectures during Her 1999 European Lecture Tour. Available in English and Chinese.

I Have Come to Take You Home

Available in Arabic, Aulacese, Bulgarian, Czech, Chinese, English, French, German, Greek, Hungarian, Indonesian, Italian, Korean, Polish, Spanish, Turkish, Romanian, and Russian.

Living in the Golden Age series

The Realization of Health – Returning to the Natural and Righteous Way of Living

Collected excerpts from the lectures of Supreme Master Ching Hai.
Available in English and Chinese.

Aphorisms

Gems of eternal wisdom from Master.
Available in English/Chinese, Spanish/Portuguese, French/German, and Korean.

The Supreme Kitchen – International Vegetarian Cuisine

A collection of culinary delicacies from all parts of the world recommended by fellow practitioners. Available in English/Chinese, Aulacese, and Japanese.

The Supreme Kitchen – Home Taste Selections

Recipes in a bilingual edition: English /Chinese.

One World... of Peace through Music

A collection of interviews and musical compositions from the 1998 benefit concert at the Shrine Auditorium in Los Angeles, California.
Trilingual edition: English/Aulacese/Chinese.

S.M. Celestial Clothes

Available in bilingual edition: English/Chinese.

The Collection of Art Creations by The Supreme Master Ching Hai – Painting Series

Through the painting of an artist, the artist's inner Self is revealed. You will be deeply touched by the intense affection, childlike innocence and motherly love of the liberated One.
Available in English and Chinese.

The Dogs in My Life (1-2)

This two-volume book set of 500 pages is a fabulous real-life set of doggy tales published by Master about Her canine companions.
Available in English and Chinese.

The Birds in My Life

In this beautifully illustrated picture-story book, Master Ching Hai shows us the secret to unlocking the animals' inner world.
Available in English and Chinese.

Poetry Collections by
The Supreme Master Ching Hai

Wu Tzu Poems
Available in Aulacese, Chinese and English.

Silent Tears
Available in English/German/French, English/Chinese, Aulacese, Spanish, Portuguese, Korean and Filipino.

The Dream of a Butterfly
Available in Aulacese, Chinese and English.

The Old Time
Available in Aulacese and English.

Pebbles and Gold
Available in Aulacese, Chinese and English.

The Lost Memories
Available in Aulacese, Chinese and English.

Traces of Previous Lives
Available in Aulacese, English and Chinese.

Traces of Previous Lives 1, 2, 3 (CD, Video, Audio tapes) Aulacese

A Path to Love Legends 1, 2, 3 (CD, Video, Audio tapes) Aulacese

Beyond the Realm of Time (CD, DVD) Aulacese

A Touch of Fragrance (CD) Aulacese

That and This Day (CD) Aulacese

Dream in the Night (CD, DVD) Aulacese

What the Hell! (CD) Aulacese

Please Keep Forever (CD) Aulacese

Songs & Compositions of The Supreme Master Ching Hai
(CD, DVD) English, Aulacese, Chinese

Song of Love
Supreme Master Ching Hai sings timeless songs in English and Aulacese
(CD, DVD) English, Aulacese

Jeweled Verses
(CD, DVD)
Song performance and poetry recitation in Aulacese by Supreme Master Ching Hai, written
by renowned Aulacese poets.

The Golden Lotus
 (CD, DVD)
We invite you to listen to the recital of Venerable Thich Man Giac's beautiful poetry, through
the melodious voice of Supreme Master Ching Hai, who also recited two of Her own poems,
"Golden Lotus" and "Sayonara".

Audio and Video Publications
Audio tapes, DVDs, music concerts DVD, CDs, MP3s and video tapes of The Supreme
Master Ching Hai's lectures and Music & Concert DVDs are available in Arabic, Armenian,
Aulacese, Bulgarian, Cantonese, Cambodia, Chinese, Croatian, Czech, Danish, Dutch,
English, Finnish, French, German, Greek, Hebrew, Hungarian, Indonesian, Italian, Japanese,
Korean, Malay, Mongolian, Nepali, Norwegian, Mandarin, Polish, Portuguese, Persian,
Russian, Romanian, Sinhalese, Slovenian, Spanish, Swedish, Thai, Turkish and Zulu.
Catalog will be sent upon request. All direct inquiries are welcome.
Please visit our bookshop's website to download our catalogue and summaries of the
contents of Master's latest publications:
http://www.smchbooks.com/ (in English and Chinese).
To order Master's publications,
please visit http://www.theCelestialShop.com to purchase online.
Or contact:
The Supreme Master Ching Hai International Association Publishing Co., Ltd., Taipei, Formosa
Tel: (886) 2-87873935 / Fax: (886) 2-87870873
E-mail: smchbooks@Godsdirectcontact.org
ROC Postal Remittance Account No.19259438 (for Formosa orders only)
Postal Account: : The Supreme Master Ching Hai International Association Publishing Co., Ltd.

Free Sample Booklet download
The Key of Immediate Enlightenment
(in 60 languages)
http://sb.godsdirectcontact.net/
http://www.direkter-kontakt-mit-gott.org/download/index.htm
http://www.Godsdirectcontact.org/sample/
http://www.Godsdirectcontact.us/com/sb/

How to Contact US

The Supreme Master Ching Hai International Association
P.O. Box 9, Hsihu Miaoli Hsien, Formosa (36899), R.O.C.
P.O.Box 730247, San Jose, CA 95173-0247, U.S.A.

Book Department
divine@Godsdirectcontact.org
Fax: 1-240-352-5613 / 886-949-883778
(You are welcome to join us in translating Master's books into other languages.)

The Supreme Master Ching Hai International Association Publishing Co., Ltd.
smchbooks@Godsdirectcontact.org
Tel: 886-2-87873935
Fax: 886-2-87870873
http://www.smchbooks.com

News Group
lovenews@Godsdirectcontact.org
Fax: 1-801-7409196 / 886-946-728475

Spiritual Information Desk
lovewish@Godsdirectcontact.org
Fax: 886-946-730699

A Journey through Aesthetic Realms TV Program Videotapes
TV@Godsdirectcontact.org
Fax: 1-413-751-0848 (USA)

S.M. Celestial Co., Ltd.

smcj@mail.sm-cj.com
Tel: 886-2-87910860
Fax: 886-2-87911216
http://www.sm-cj.com

Celestial Shop

http://www.theCelestialShop.com
http://www.edenrules.com

Quan Yin WWW Sites

God's direct contact—The Supreme Master Ching Hai International Association's global Internet:
http://www.Godsdirectcontact.org.tw/eng/links/links.htm

This portal provides a directory of links to Quan Yin Web sites in a variety of languages, as well as 24-hour access to the TV program *A Journey through Aesthetic Realms*. You may also download multilingual editions of *The Key of Immediate Enlightenment Sample Booklet*, or download or subscribe to *The Supreme Master Ching Hai News* available in eBook or printable format, or simply browse the sites' contents online.

Supreme Master Television

Info@SupremeMasterTV.com
Tel: 1-626-444-4385
Fax: 1-626-444-4386
http://www.suprememastertv.com/

Supreme Master Television goes GLOBAL on NOV. 16, 2007
Launching on 10 NEW Satellite Platforms!
Enjoy positive, inspirational and entertaining programs
With over 30 languages and subtitles!
Free-to-Air Satellite TV channel
Also LIVE online www.SupremeMasterTV.com

Master thanks **the following individual**
for their meticulous assistance:

Steven André, T. June, Vian Hang *(Cameramen)*

Gary Lai, Annie Yu, Nadir Yen, Eve Lin, Pearl Huang, Kim Jung Eun, An So Young, Sofia and Jackie *(Design and Layout)*

Wang Bor Tang, Yu Hui-Chun, Gary Lai, Sofia, Luisa and Nadir Yen *(Graphic Design)*

Lynn McGee, Evelyn, Jane Chu, Sun Wang, Elaine Lin, Grace Liang and Becky Chen, Sing and Moon *(Copy Proofreading)*

"Your love and dedication
will flower more enjoyment
in the garden of the heart."

~ Supreme Master Ching Hai

The Dogs in My Life

The Supreme Master Ching Hai

The Dogs in My Life

> " I hope to let the readers enjoy some glimpse of the beautiful ways that dogs walk the Earth with us, and through them, understand more about other beings. "
> ~ Supreme Master Ching Hai

Hardcover
Book (1) : 268 pages
Book (2) : 274 pages
Size : 21cm x 28cm

In the newly released *The Dogs in My Life* (Volumes 1 & 2), the first publication lovingly written and personally designed by Supreme Master Ching Hai, readers will re-discover the simplicity of love and rejoice in the sincerity of friendship, as exhibited by the 10 canine friends, with names like Benny, Lucky, Happy, Goody, and Hermit. Learn about the Scholar, Fruity, Princissa, Chip Ahoy, the Shadow Hunter, and others; listen to their engaging tales. They all have diverse life stories and distinctive personalities, yet their devotion for their "human pet" is unequivocal, and their humor, intelligence and many other noble qualities are truly from the same source.

Read *The Dogs in My Life*, and fall in love with some the most special beings on Earth.

Contact our Publishing Company:
The Supreme Master Ching Hai International Association Publishing Co., Ltd.   No 236 Soungshan Road, Taipei, Formosa, R. O. C.
Tel: 886-2-87873935 Fax: 886-2-87870873 www.smchbooks.com E-mail:smchbooks@Godsdirectcontact.org

Alternative Living

We Pray for You

Change Your Life
Change Your Heart
Change Your Diet

♥~~~♥

No more killing
Be healthy and loving

Save our Lives!
We Love You

Examples of nutritious, life saving food:

Foods	Protein Concentration (Percentage by Weight)
Tofu (from soya)	16 %
Gluten (from flour)	70 %
Corn	13 %
Rice	8.6 %
Soy beans, kidney beans, chick peas, lentils, etc.	10 - 35 %
Almonds, walnuts, cashews, hazel nuts, pine nuts, etc.	14 - 30 %
Pumpkin seeds, sesame seeds, sunflower seeds, etc.	18 - 24 %

- Concentrated multi-vitamin tablets/capsules are also a good source of vitamins, minerals and anti-oxidants.
- Fruits and vegetables are full of vitamins, minerals and anti-oxidants and contain high-quality fiber for maintaining good health and a long life.
- The recommended daily allowance: 50 grams of protein (Average adult).
- Calcium from vegetables is more absorbable than from cow's milk.

- **To diminish the real threat of a worldwide pandemic from bird flu,**
- **To avoid the danger of mad cow disease (BSE) and pig disease (PMWS), etc.**
- **To stop the continuing gruesome sacrifice of billions of our sweet domestic animals, marine life and feathered friends daily,**

It's wise to change to a vegetarian diet for good.

It's Health
It's Economy
It's Ecology
It's Compassion
It's Peace
It's Noble

Long Life to You!

Thank You for Your Compassion

For more information, please refer to the websites listed below:
http://AL.Godsdirectcontact.org.tw/ or e-mail to AL@Godsdirectcontact.org
http://www.vegsoc.org/ http://www.vrg.org/ http://www.vegsource.com/
**Supreme Master Television, airing only positive programming,
will bring a new dimension into your life.**
Available worldwide as 24-hour live Internet TV at:
http://suprememastertv.com/webtv/

Vegetarian and Vegan Elite of the World :

Philosophers, Spiritual Leaders
Paramahansa Yogananda *(Indian Spiritual Teacher)*, **Socrates** *(Greek philosopher)*, **Jesus Christ & early Christians**, **Confucius** *(Chinese philosopher)*, **Shakyamuni Buddha, Lao Tzu** *(Chinese Philosopher)*, **St. Francis of Assisi** *(Italian Christian Saint)*, **Thich Nhat Hanh** *(Vietnamese Buddhist monk\writer)*, **Yogi Maharishi Mahesh** *(Indian writer, philosopher, leader of Transcendental Meditation)*, **Leo Nikolayevich Tolstoy** *(Russian philosopher)*, **Pythagoras** *(Greek mathematician/philosopher)*, **Zoroaster** *(Iranian - Founder of Zoroastrianism)*, **Muhammad Al-Ghazali** *(Iranian Islamic scholar and Sufi Saint)*, **Muhammad Rahiim Bawa Muhaiyadeen** *(Sri Lankan Islamic author and Sufi Saint)*, **Bulleh Shah** *(Muslim Sufi Saint)*, **Etc.**

Writers, Artists & Painters
Leonardo Da Vinci *(Italian painter)*, **Ralph Waldo Emerson** *(US essayist, and poet)*, **George Bernard Shaw** *(Irish writer)*, **John Robbins** *(US writer)*, **Mark Twain** *(US writer)*, **Albert Schweitzer** *(German philosopher, physician, musician)*, **Plutarch** *(Greek writer)*, **Voltaire** *(French writer)*, **Sadegh Hedayat** *(Iranian novelist)*, **Etc.**

Scientists, Inventors & Engineers
Charles Darwin *(British naturalist)*, **Albert Einstein** *(German Scientist)*, **Thomas Edison** *(US scientist/inventor)*, **Sir Isaac Newton** *(British scientist)*, **Nikola Tesla** *(Serbian-American scientist/inventor)*, **Henry Ford** *(US Founder of Ford Motors)*, **Etc.**

Politicians, Statespersons and Activists
Susan B. Anthony *(US leader of Woman's Suffrage movement)*, **Mahatma Gandhi** *(Indian Civil Rights leader)*, **Coretta Scott King** *(American Civil Rights activist and leader, wife of Dr. Martin Luther King Jr.)*, **President Janez Drnovsek of Slovenia**, **Dr. A. P. J. Abdul Kalam** *(President of India)*, **Dr. Manmohan Singh** *(Prime Minister of India)*, **Dennis J. Kucinich** *(US Congressman)*, **Etc.**

Actors, Film stars & TV Stars
Pamela Anderson *(US actress)*, **Ashley Judd** *(US actress)*, **Brigitte Bardot** *(French actress)*, **John Cleese** *(British actor)*, **David Duchovny** *(US actor)*, **Danny Devito** *(US actor)*, **Cameron Diaz** *(US actress)*, **Richard Gere** *(US actor)*, **Daryl Hannah** *(US actress)*, **Dustin Hoffman** *(US actor)*, **Katie Holmes** *(US actress)*, **Steve Martin** *(US actor)*, **Demi Moore** *(US actress)*, **Ian McKellen** *(British actor)*, **Tobey Maguire** *(US actor)*, **Paul Newman** *(US actor)*, **Gwyneth Paltrow** *(US actress)*, **Joaquin Phoenix** *(US actor)*, **Steven Seagal** *(US actor)*, **Brooke Shields** *(US model/actress)*, **Jerry Seinfeld** *(US actor)*, **Naomi Watts** *(US actress)*, **Kate Winslet** *(British actress)*, **Etc.**

Pop stars & Musicians
Joan Baez *(US folk singer)*, **George Harrison** *(British musician, member of the Beatles)*, **Paul McCartney** *(British musician, member of the Beatles)*, **Ringo Starr** *(British musician, member of the Beatles)*, **Bob Dylan** *(US musician)*, **Michael Jackson** *(US pop star)*, **Morrissey** *(British singer)*, **Olivia Newton John** *(British-Australian singer)*, **Sinead O'Connor** *(Irish singer)*, **Pink** *(US singer)*, **Prince** *(US pop star)*, **Justin Timberlake** *(US pop singer)*, **Tina Turner** *(US pop star)*, **Shania Twain** *(Canadian singer)*, **Vanessa Williams** *(US pop singer)*, **Etc.**

Sports Personalities
Billie Jean King *(US Tennis champion)*, **Bill Walton** *(US Basketball player)*, **Carl Lewis** *(US 9-time Olympic Gold-Medalist in Track & Field)*, **Edwin C. Moses** *(US 2-time Gold-Medalist in Track & Field)*, **Elena Walendzik** *(German Boxing champion)*, **Alexander Dargatz** *(German Athlete, Body-building champion, physician)*, **Etc.**

Models
Christie Brinkley *(US supermodel)*, **Christy Turlington** *(US supermodel)*, **Etc.**

And the list goes on... http://AL.Godsdirectcontact.org.tw/vg-vip

The Birds in My Life

Inspired by the birds
Compiled by:
Supreme Master Ching Hai

Cameramen:
Supreme Master Ching Hai / Steven André / T. June / Vian Hang

Design and Layout:
Gary Lai, Annie Yu, Nadir Yen, Eve Lin, Pearl Huang (from Formosa);
Kim Jung Eun and An So Young (from Korea); Sofia and Jackie (from Hsihu)

Graphic Design:
Wang Bor Tang, Yu Hui-Chun, Gary Lai and Nadir Yen (from Formosa); Sofia and Luisa (from Hsihu)

Copy Proofreading:
Lynn McGee, Evelyn and Jane Chu (from USA);
Sun Wang, Elaine Lin, Grace Liang and Becky Chen (from Formosa); Sing and Moon (from Hsihu)

Publisher:
The Supreme Master Ching Hai International Association Publishing Co., Ltd.
No 236 Soungshan Road, Taipei, Formosa, R. O. C.
Tel: 886-2-87873935
Fax: 886-2-87870873
www.smchbooks.com

The Supreme Master Ching Hai©2007
First Edition First Print: June 2007
First Edition Second Print: July 2007
Second Edition First Print: October 2007
Second Edition Second Print: November 2007
Printed in Formosa
ISBN: 978-986-6895-14-2